real- ... es

LIV
CHERNOBYL

Ira's Story

by Linda Walker

Produced in association with

Chernobyl Children's Project (UK)

WE WOULD LIKE TO THANK THE FOLLOWING FOR THEIR HELP IN THE PRODUCTION OF THIS BOOK:

Linda Walker, Liena Fedarchuk, Helen Walker, Mags Whiting, Glenda Norris and Glenda Tracey of Chernobyl Children's Project (UK); Dr Ian Fairlie (Consultant on Radiation in the Environment); The teachers, carers and children of the Zhuravichi Children's Home, Belarus; The teachers, carers and children of the Rechitsa Boarding School, Belarus; Jean Coppendale and Indexing Specialists (UK) Ltd;

and our special thanks to

Ira

without whom this book would not have been possible.

Picture credits: t=top; b=bottom; c=centre; l=left; r=right; OFC=outside front cover; OBC=outside back cover.
Chernobyl Children's Project (UK) – Linda Walker: OFC, 1, 3, 5l, 7l, 8, 9b, 11, 12, 13tl, 14, 15t, 16, 17, 18, 19, 20, 21, 22, 23, 24, 25, 26, 27, 28, 29, 30, 31, 32, 33, 34, 35, 36, 37, 38–39, 40, 41, 43bl, 44, 45. Corbis: 9t, 42.
Getty images: 10. Magnum: 6bl, 13bl, 15br. Photos12: 5br. Every effort has been made to trace the copyright holders, and we apologise in advance for any unintentional omissions. We would be pleased to insert the appropriate acknowledgements in any subsequent edition of this publication.

THE INTERVIEWERS

The interviews with Ira (the subject of the book) were conducted by Linda Walker, the national co-ordinator of the British charity Chernobyl Children's Project (UK), and Liena Fedarchuk who works as the Director of CCP (UK)'s work in Gomel. CCP (UK) has been working in Belarus since 1995 helping children affected by the Chernobyl nuclear accident.

HOW IRA WAS CHOSEN

Linda says: *"During my work in Belarus with CCP (UK), I have met many children who have suffered serious illnesses and disabilities, and terrible hardships as a result of the 1986 Chernobyl disaster. I have known Ira since she was nine years old, and chose her as the subject for this book because her severe disabilities, and the limited life she has led, have not dimmed her spirit."*

THE INTERVIEW PROCESS

The interviews held in November, 2004, with Ira, her friends, teachers and carers were carried out in Russian by Liena Fedarchuk. The interview text was then translated into English. Linda Walker, the members of CCP (UK) and Ira's friends, carers and teachers have many memories of Ira and have helped to explain parts of her story that she does not remember.

CONTENTS

Introduction

In the early hours of Saturday, 26 April 1986, the world's worst nuclear accident happened at the Chernobyl power station, in the Ukraine. Over the following days a disaster would unfold that was to have terrible, long-term consequences for the people of the Ukraine, Belarus and western Russia.

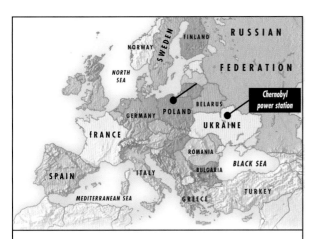

The Chernobyl power station is situated 100 km north of the Ukrainian capital, Kiev, and 12 km south of the border with Belarus.

A NIGHTMARE SITUATION

At the time of the Chernobyl accident, the Ukraine, Belarus and Russia were part of the Soviet Union. Along with many other Soviet states, the Ukraine relied on nuclear power to supply a significant amount of the country's electricity. On the night of the 26 April, a potentially dangerous safety check on the cooling system of the No. 4 reactor at the Chernobyl power station was carried out by an inexperienced operating crew. During the test, a sudden power surge caused the reactor to reach 100 times its normal power in a matter of seconds. The emergency shutdown failed and then the worst thing possible happened – the crew lost control of the reactor.

Power levels and temperatures inside the reactor rose, causing a massive explosion.

The reactor building's 1,000-tonne sealing cap was blown off and a lethal shower of radioactive material was launched 1,500 metres into the air. As temperatures inside the reactor soared to over 2,000°C, the reactor's protective graphite covering ignited, creating a poisonous, blazing inferno.

THE FIRST CHERNOBYL VICTIMS

In the days that followed the accident, hundreds of soldiers and men from the power station's fire and operating crews were drafted in to fight the blaze. However, both the power-station management and the Soviet authorities were unprepared for a disaster of this magnitude, and the men were not issued with any breathing apparatus or protective clothing. Some of the firefighters were to receive doses of radiation up to 13,000 times higher than the maximum annual dose recommended by the European Union for people who live near a nuclear power plant. Beyond any medical help, many of the men fell ill and some died within weeks of the accident.

For 10 days the fire continued to burn, propelling radioactive particles into the atmosphere. Finally, on the May 6, the blaze was extinguished, and the radioactive emissions were brought under control.

A SECRET DISASTER

As with many aspects of life in the Soviet Union, the Chernobyl disaster was immediately shrouded in secrecy. The Soviet authorities were afraid of creating a panic and hoped to keep this huge failure in their nuclear programme a secret. Officials in Moscow insisted there had only been a small accident and that there was no threat to the health of the population.

The reluctance of the Soviet authorities to admit to the scale of the disaster, caused serious delays in advising ordinary people how to protect themselves in the aftermath of the accident.

A memorial, in Bragin, Belarus, to the firemen who died as a result of the Chernobyl accident.

CHERNOBYL TIMELINE

21/12/83: Chernobyl reactor No. 4 goes on stream ahead of schedule, but with many safety tests not completed.

26/4/86: Chernobyl reactor No. 4 runs out of control during a safety test and explodes.

28/4/86: A Danish nuclear research laboratory announces there has been a maximum credible accident at Chernobyl. Government-run Moscow TV tells the Soviet people that an accident has occurred at Chernobyl. No details are given.

26/4/86–5/5/86: Wind and rain spread radiation over the Ukraine, Belarus, western Russia and parts of Europe. 1,800 helicopter flights deposit 5,000 tonnes of lead and sand onto the burning reactor to smother the fire and absorb the radiation.

UP TO 6/5/86: The reactor is cooled by liquid nitrogen pumped beneath it. The fire is extinguished. Radioactive releases stop.

The timeline continues on page 7.

May 1986: A power station worker checks radiation levels while flying over the destroyed No. 4 reactor in a helicopter.

The red arrow shows the path of the radioactive cloud as winds carried it north in the first few days after the accident.

WHAT IS NUCLEAR POWER?

Nuclear power has been used to produce electricity since the 1950s. The power is produced by a process called nuclear fission: a chain reaction in which radioactive atoms shoot out neutrons which split other atoms. This process produces energy in the form of heat.

Inside a nuclear reactor, fuel rods made from uranium (a radioactive element) are placed in the reactor's core. The rods are close enough for their neutrons to strike each other. As the atoms in the fuel rods split apart, the rods heat up, heating the cooling water around them which then turns to steam. The steam powers turbines which spin to produce electricity.

EVACUATIONS

On April 27, 36 hours after the accident, 45,000 people were evacuated from Pripyat, a settlement just 3 km from Chernobyl. Over the next 10 days, a 30 km exclusion zone was set up around the power station and a further 130,000 people were evacuated from their homes in 76 towns and villages.

IN THE PATH OF THE CLOUD

To the north of the Ukraine lies Belarus, a beautiful country of large forests, marshlands, lakes, rivers and farms. In the days following the accident, winds carried huge clouds of radioactive particles north, depositing an estimated 70 per cent of the Chernobyl fallout onto Belarus. Some areas, such as Gomel in southern Belarus, became as severely contaminated as pieces of land in the immediate vicinity of the Chernobyl reactor. Localised heavy rain showers resulted in radioactive 'hotspots' hundreds of kilometres from the plant.

The town of Pripyat was built to house Chernobyl workers and their families. Today it is still deserted because of dangerous levels of radiation.

Even today, many people living in rural areas of Belarus still use a horse and cart as their main form of transportation.

LIVING FROM THE LAND

Belarus has a population of 10 million people and is one of the poorest countries in Europe. Belarussian people live on low incomes (the average annual income is USD $1300) with many relying on food they grow or produce themselves. Following the Chernobyl disaster, people continued to consume home-grown vegetables, milk from cows that had eaten contaminated grass, wild berries and fungi, unaware that they were eating and drinking radioactive substances.

It would be many weeks before they were warned by the authorities that locally produced food could be dangerously contaminated.

EXTENDING THE DANGER ZONE

Over time, a belief that the radioactive contamination simply stopped at the 30 km exclusion zone developed. It was 1989 before accurate maps of the fallout area were issued by Pravda (the main Soviet newspaper).

The maps showed that some areas 300 km to the north of the Chernobyl plant were equally as contaminated as those inside the 30 km exclusion zone. A second series of evacuations began.

CHERNOBYL TIMELINE

15/11/86: A 272,000-tonne reinforced, concrete building, to contain reactor No.4, is completed.

NOVEMBER 1986: Chernobyl reactors1 and 2 return to operation.

DECEMBER 1987: Reactor No.3, which was damaged by the explosion,is repaired and back in operation.

20/4/89: The Soviet government halts construction work on the Chernobyl reactors No. 5 and No. 6.

1991: The Soviet Union falls and the Ukraine, Belarus and Russia become independent countries, inheriting all the financial, economical, social and health problems caused by the disaster.

1993: A thyroid centre is established in Gomel by the Otto Hug Strahleninstitut, Munich.

5/7/00: US$715 million is pledged by the G7 countries, the EU and the Ukraine to build a new shelter for reactor No. 4.

12/12/00: The Chernobyl nuclear power station is closed down.

APRIL 2001: At the 'Fifteen years after Chernobyl Accident – Lessons Learned' conference in Kiev, a direct link between the accident and thyroid cancer in children is internationally recognised.

2001: Scientists and radiation experts from around the world call for further research into the links between the Chernobyl accident, genetic abnormalities and medical conditions such as cancer.

CHAPTER ONE: A Chernobyl Baby

Following the Chernobyl accident, there has been a significant increase in the number of people in parts of Belarus, the Ukraine and Russia suffering from serious illnesses. Many of the worst affected are children. Most experts now agree that the increase in conditions such as cancer, heart disease and diabetes is linked to the exposure to radiation that the people of the Chernobyl region suffered. Exposure to radiation also carries another hidden cost. In the areas contaminated by the radioactive fallout, the number of babies born with physical or mental disabilities has risen.

LINDA WALKER SAYS ...

"Ira was born just two years after the Chernobyl disaster, in a village called Tihinichi in the north of the Gomel Region. Gomel is the most contaminated part of Belarus and there has been an estimated 80 per cent rise in the number

January 2005: Linda Walker catches up with Ira on a visit to Rechitsa Boarding School in Gomel, Belarus. Ira has lived at Rechitsa since 2003.

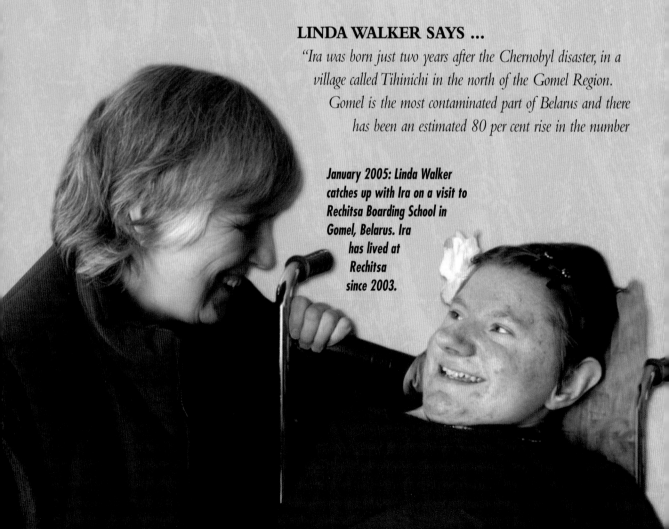

of children born with disabilities in this area since the Chernobyl accident.

Ira was born with damage to all her limbs: her legs are very short and her feet twist inwards; her arms are also short and her left hand twists outwards. Her disabilities were very likely caused by her mother's exposure to radiation.

Members of Chernobyl Children's Project (UK) first met Ira when she was nine years old. When we toured the cots full of disabled children on our visits to the Zhuravichi Children's Home in Gomel, Ira would always have a bright smile for us. However, it would be two years before we learned the full extent of how intelligent she was.

For 11 years, Ira spent almost all her time lying in a cot with nothing to do and little or no stimulation.

But Ira has huge strength of character – all she needed was to be given a chance."

RADIATION AND CANCER

Cancers form when the body's cells begin to multiply abnormally, producing cell masses called tumours. Nuclear radiation is carcinogenic which means it increases the chances of the body's cells behaving in this way. Since the Chernobyl accident, doctors in the affected regions have reported an increase in the number of brain tumours, cases of leukaemia and other cancers.

This young boy has been receiving chemotherapy treatment for cancer. One side effect of the treatment is hair loss.

A doctor in Gomel treats a child with cancer. The majority of thyroid cancer sufferers are children and young people.

THYROID CANCER

In the years following the accident, there has been a dramatic increase in the incidence of thyroid cancer across Belarus. The thyroid gland in the neck takes in and stores iodine which is needed by the body. However, during the Chernobyl accident, radioactive iodine was released into the atmosphere. This radioactive iodine was taken in by children's thyroid glands and stored, eventually causing cancer. Thyroid cancer is normally treated successfully, often by the surgical removal of the thyroid gland, which leaves the patient requiring medication for the rest of their life.

"When Ira was born with such severe disabilities her mother must have been deeply shocked. In the Soviet Union, at the time when Ira was born, attitudes towards children with disabilities were very much as they were in Britain in Victorian times. Children, like Soviet society, were supposed to be perfect. If they had obvious disabilities they were a source of deep embarrassment and fathers, in particular, were not willing to bring up a disabled child as part of their family.

Doctors normally advised the mothers of even mildly disabled babies to give their children away. In Ira's case, the doctors may have genuinely believed that she would not survive for long, as she must have been very tiny and weak. The mother of an autistic child born 14 years ago, puts it like this, 'When my son was born I had two choices. I could put him in an institution and throw his life away. Or I could keep him with me and throw my life away.' There were no other options available to desperate mothers at that time.

Today, there are many associations of parents in Belarus helping each other to support their disabled children. They persuade the government to do more to help and work with foreign partners. Sixteen years ago, there were no such associations and there would have been nowhere for Ira's mother to turn for help if she had considered trying to keep her baby.

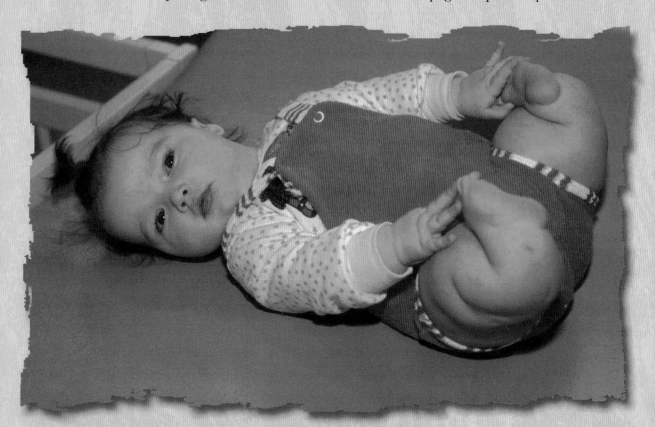

This little girl was born with deformities to her legs and feet. She was born in Belarus six years after the Chernobyl accident. There are no photographs in existence of Ira as a baby or toddler.

So, Ira was given away to the Abandoned Babies' Home in Gomel. Natalia, one of Ira's carers at the Zhuravichi Children's Home (where Ira went to live when she was four years old), told us, 'Ira's family and parents never came to visit her and never contacted the orphanage about her. We think the mother rejected her in the maternity hospital as Ira was born very disabled."

This little boy at the Abandoned Babies' Home was born with hydrocephalus – an accumulation of fluid in the brain which makes the head enlarge. The condition can cause mental disabilities.

BIRTH DEFECTS

Levels of radiation that are too low to kill a human body cell, can still cause damage by disrupting the DNA – the genetic material that is stored in the cell and determines what a living thing will be like when it grows. Radiation damage to egg or sperm cells, can lead to abnormalities in any children that are conceived, not just in the current generation, but in future generations too. If a woman is exposed to radiation during pregnancy, the foetus may die, or the baby may be born with disabilities.

THE ABANDONED BABIES' HOME

Today, there are still over 100 babies and young children living at the Abandoned Babies' Home in Gomel. Around 40 of the children have disabilities such as Down's Syndrome, autism, cerebral palsy, spina bifida, hydrocephalus or microcephalus, missin limbs or severe learning disabilities.

The babies at the home who are not disabled, have normally been born to young, single mothers or families who are too poor to keep them. These children are likely to be adopted either in Belarus or abroad, but it is very rare for a child with a disability to be adopted or even fostered.

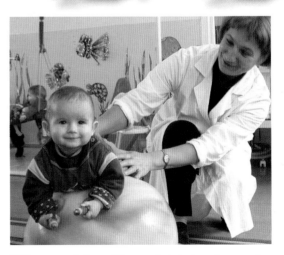

With overseas help, conditions at the baby home have vastly improved since the 1980s. It is a brighter, better equipped place with professionally trained carers.

CHAPTER TWO: Life at Zhuravichi

After four years at the Abandoned Babies' Home, Ira was moved to the Zhuravichi Children's Home, a huge institution hidden deep in the Gomel countryside. Over 200 children, with a wide range of physical and mental disabilities, were living at Zhuravichi.

LINDA WALKER SAYS ...

"It took Chernobyl Children's Project (UK) several months to discover where the most disabled children were sent when they left the baby home in Gomel.

When we first visited Zhuravichi most of the rooms were bare and gloomy and it was quite a depressing place. The children were kept clean, dressed and fed, but for many of them, especially the 50 who were living in cots, that was about it. There were very few toys, wheelchairs or disability aids, and no bean bags or comfy mats where children from the cots could spend some time out of bed.

For intelligent children who could not walk, life was especially bleak at Zhuravichi. Their physical disabilities meant they were regarded as being unable to learn. They had very little to occupy their time and no opportunities to learn to read.

Ira had been put into a large room with 20 very disabled children, the majority of whom had severe learning difficulties as well as their physical problems. All the children, including Ira, spent their days just lying in their cots."

IRA SAYS ...

"I can't remember much about my life when I used to lie in the cot all the time. I do remember hearing children crying a lot and one carer who was very kind and

The Zhuravichi Children's Home. When Ira went to live there in 1992, almost no-one in Belarus knew that such homes existed.

A small, wooden house in Tihinichi, the village where Ira was born. Many poorer homes in Belarus had no running water and families had to collect their water from a well.

friendly, but I have forgotten her name. She used to talk to me about her family, and I wished she was my mum. I liked it when I had a bath, the feeling of warm water, and being sleepy afterwards."

In the Belarus village of Maiski, women harvest potatoes grown close to the 30 km exclusion zone. Poor families had no option but to continue to eat food they had grown in contaminated soil.

A COUNTRY IN CRISIS

With the break-up of the Soviet Union in 1991, the newly independent government of Belarus was left to manage the aftermath of the Chernobyl disaster. The authorities struggled to cope with the costs of moving people away from the most contaminated areas, building accommodation for the evacuees and providing uncontaminated food and proper healthcare.

• Life for ordinary people in Belarus was also much harder after Chernobyl. People lived with the constant anxiety that they or their children would fall ill from exposure to radiation.

• Families evacuated from contaminated areas were often moved from country villages to specially built high-rise blocks in the cities.

• For many families it was a great wrench to leave family graves behind in the exclusion zone. In Belarus it is customary to live near to where your parents and grandparents are buried.

• Re-settlers found it hard to fit in and find jobs in the cities they moved to. They lived with the stigma of radioactive contamination, which many people regarded as an infectious disease.

• Children evacuated from affected areas were bullied in their new schools and called 'the Chernobyls'.

LINDA WALKER SAYS ...

"In the early 1990s, institutions such as Zhuravichi were a low priority for the government of Belarus. The budget of an orphanage like Zhuravichi provided for the staff salaries, heating, simple food and basic clothes for the children, but very little else. The carers at the orphanage worked hard to look after the children, but they had to work long hours, and were poorly paid. They had no time or energy to give the children the attention they craved. Some of the more capable children were trained in craft skills, but most of the children did not have any lessons.

We would walk around the cot rooms, moving sadly from bed to bed. Some of the children had twisted limbs, some were blind, a few had severe breathing problems. From some of the children we could get a smile or even giggles by making a fuss of them. Others looked at us quite blankly and some were frightened by the presence of strangers.

It was always a pleasure to get to Ira's bed and see her smile as soon as we spoke to her. Like all the children living in the cots, Ira needed to wear a nappy. Proper nappies, either towelling or disposable, were seldom available, so the children often had to wear pieces of cloth which were not very absorbent.

When Ira was quite small, probably nine years old, one of the carers told us that she was so delicate, it caused her pain to have her clothes changed or to be taken for a bath. Ira does not remember this, and as she grew bigger, she became stronger and healthier and could be lifted and moved without any problems."

Ira in her cot at Zhuravichi. She is about nine years old.

14

1998: a group of the Zhuravichi children. Ira's best friend at Zhuravichi, Vova, is on the far right of the photograph.

HOW LONG WILL THE CONTAMINATION LAST?

The most significant radionuclides released at Chernobyl were iodine-131, caesium-137 and strontium-90. Radionuclides decay at different rates: for example, eight days after the accident, the level of radioactivity of the iodine-131 had already halved. This is called the nuclide's 'half-life'. After another eight days, the amount halved again to leave a quarter of the original dose. Nearly 20 years on, the radioactivity levels of iodine-131 are now tiny. However, caesium-137 and strontium-90 have half-lives of 30 years. This means it will take over 300 years for the levels of radioactivity to reach safer levels. Caesium-137 is transported to muscular tissue throughout the body, while strontium-90 is deposited in the bones.

THE DECONTAMINATION PLAN

At first, it was believed that it would be possible to 'clean up' the contaminated areas close to the Chernobyl power station. The Soviet authorities conscripted 800,000 men to work as 'liquidators'. The men worked for periods of up to six months. They scraped the top soil from areas such as school playgrounds, washed down the roofs and walls of buildings and even demolished contaminated houses. However, the decontamination plan did not work. The towns and villages in the 30 km exclusion zone remained seriously contaminated. The Russian, Ukrainian and Belarussian authorities say that to date, 25,000 of the men used as liquidators have died from radiation-related illnesses.

Nikolai Yanchen was a conscripted liquidator. He lost his right leg to cancer and now lives in a small village near the 30 km danger zone.

GLENDA NORRIS SAYS ...

"I spent two months as a CCP (UK) volunteer at Zhuravichi in 1998. Most of my time was devoted to getting children out of the cots and giving them the chance to move around a little.

Ira was not allowed to spend much time out of her cot, so I tried to think of ways to entertain her where she was. She was always pleased to see me, but I don't speak Russian so I could not communicate with her much. I had a tapestry of the alphabet – British, not Russian – and I hung that above her bed, and taught her the first few letters. Within a week she had learned most of the alphabet. She was so anxious to learn and so happy when I praised her skill. It was a joy to work with her."

Ira aged 11 years with Glenda Norris who volunteered with CCP (UK) in 1998 to 2000, and worked with Ira at Zhuravichi.

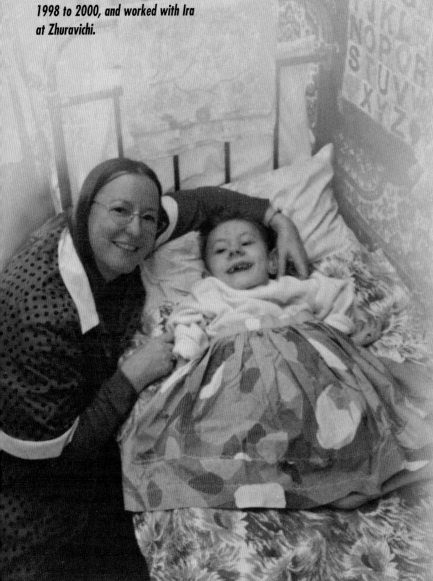

IRA SAYS ...

"It was always a special day when visitors came. The carers would make sure everyone was ready for the visit. If they suggested that I should wear a pretty dress, I was always very happy. Some days we had to wait hours before the visitors came to our room. When they came to my cot I always felt very excited. I knew Mags and Linda best. They would say, 'Kraseeva' (beautiful) and I thought, they mean me!

Glenda came to see me nearly every day when she was staying at Zhuravichi. After a while she put a big cloth on the wall with letters on it. She taught me a few letters every day, and I would lie in bed looking at them and trying to remember them."

MAGS WHITING SAYS ...

"Ira had always been special to me. She was the same age as my grand-daughter and one Christmas, when Ira was nine, I wrote a poem about her comparing Stephanie's happy, busy Christmas with the lonely time Ira would have. On every visit to Zhuravichi I looked forward to seeing Ira, with her radiant smile. But I thought perhaps she was happy because she did not understand very much.

Then, one day, Glenda Norris took Linda Walker and me to Ira's cot and said, 'Look what she can do!' With a beam from ear to ear, Ira read for us, 'ay, bee, cee, dee, ...' almost all the way through the alphabet. I told her how clever she was. Then I turned away so she would not see the tears in my eyes."

Mags Whiting is a trustee of Chernobyl Children's Project (UK).

Mags Whiting plays with children in the Zhuravichi playground which was built by CCP (UK) in 2001.

A CLOSED INSTITUTION

During the Soviet era, Zhuravichi was a closed institution and no-one was allowed to visit the children who lived there. When Ira first went to live at Zhuravichi in 1992, the home had 200 members of staff: cleaners, cooks, maintenance staff and carers. However, most of the carers were untrained, and many did not even have a particular desire to work with children – they were local people and there were few other jobs nearby.

ZHURAVICHI TODAY

In the past ten years, with the support of foreign partners and three Polish nuns who have lived at the home for over six years, the staff have transformed the children's environment. There are now many toys and mobility aids, a physiotherapy room, a playground accessible to disabled children, and new toilets and bathrooms. Proper training has been arranged for the staff, and there are lessons and summer holidays for the children.

LINDA WALKER SAYS ...

"When Ira's friends from the UK realised what a bright child she was, it seemed all the more tragic that she should be condemned to lie in a cot all day.

Ira at 11 years old in the spring of 1999. This was the first year she was put in a wheelchair. She is with one of the girls at Zhuravichi, Tanya.

In 1999, CCP (UK) brought wheelchairs to Zhuravichi and Ira was able to sit up for the first time in her life.

From her cot Ira had seen nothing but a white ceiling. Once she was in the wheelchair she could spend a few hours every day watching and talking to the people around her. However, Ira still only had tantalising glimpses of sky and the tops of trees through the high windows in her room. So, one warm summer day, Ira was taken outside for the first time."

IRA SAYS ...

"When I was first taken out of my cot and placed in a wheelchair I was frightened. It felt so strange to be upright without a carer holding on to me. Once I realised I was safe, I felt very excited to be able to see all around me. Instead of having a quick look around as I was carried to the bath, I was able to look for as long as I liked at everything in my room. I could even sit in the corridor and watch children from other rooms coming and going for lunch, or going to lessons.

Some days were special because we celebrated birthdays. We would all go to the gym and some of the children would sing. We had sweets to eat and then we would have a disco. It was wonderful!

The first time I went outside, Vova pushed me and we went out into the garden. The sun was bright and hot, so we went to sit under the trees. I saw the cows in the field nearby

Luba the Zhuravichi physiotherapist tries some new equipment with Stas. Occupational therapists and physiotherapists from the UK trained the carers at Zhuravichi how to use mobility aids, such as walking frames.

and I heard some birds singing. I watched the children playing and felt the fresh air on my face." (Vova was Ira's best friend at Zhuravichi.)

LINDA WALKER SAYS ...

"In the Spring of 2001, a CCP (UK) aid convoy delivered a variety of walking frames and special seats to Zhuravichi. These had all been donated by schools and hospitals in the UK, in some cases because they had acquired more modern equipment. A team of therapists from Devon spent several days at Zhuravichi. They fitted the physically disabled children into the most appropriate seats, and showed the staff how to use the mobility aids."

CONTAMINATED BELARUS

For many of the most severely disabled Zhuravichi children, 1999 was the first time in their lives they had been able to go outside. While they enjoyed the sunshine and 'fresh' air, 13 years on from the Chernobyl accident, the environment around Zhuravichi was still badly contaminated by radioactive fallout.

• People living in many villages in the Gomel region received more than a lifetime's 'safe dose' of radiation within three to four years of the accident. It has been estimated that southern Belarus was exposed to radioactivity 90 times greater than that released by the Hiroshima atomic bomb.

• In 1986, the average life expectancy in Belarus was 72.6 years, by 2000 it had dropped to 67.6 years.

• By 2000, the air was considered safe, but dust lifted by ploughing or wind erosion could put radiation back into the air at any time.

• One quarter of the farmland and one fifth of the forests in Belarus were poisoned by radioactive contamination.

• Some areas are contaminated with plutonium which has a half-life of 24,000 years.

A forest area inside the exclusion zone. Summer forest fires can still spread radiation.

CHAPTER THREE: Dreams & New Goals

Most of the children at Zhuravichi had never had a holiday or even been outside the grounds of the orphanage. So, Chernobyl Children's Project (UK) decided to organise a holiday in Belarus for as many children as possible.

LINDA WALKER SAYS ...

"A few of the children from Zhuravichi had been to Italy to stay with families, but rather than take a few more abroad, we decided it would be best to try to arrange a holiday in Belarus for as many children as possible. We found a sanatorium, or holiday camp, in a clean part of the country, where the Director was willing to accept disabled children, and we persuaded the local authority to pay part of the cost. Raisa Ivanovna, the Director at Zhuravichi, was asked to choose about 80 children who would get the most benefit from a holiday.

Unfortunately, Ira was not one of the children selected to go to the holiday camp. Doctors who visited Zhuravichi said she was too delicate and it would be too risky for her to travel.

When her friends set off for camp, Ira dreamed of going to the sanatorium holiday with them.

Ludmilla Markovna is a teacher at Zhuravichi. During the interviews for this book, Ludmilla told us, 'All the

Ira with her best friend Vova in 1999.

children live on their memories of the sanatorium all the year round. They enjoy it and often talk about it. They want to go to sanatorium holidays as they make new contacts and have so many new experiences. It is like a window into real life.'"

IRA SAYS ...

"I felt upset when my friends and all the other children went to the holiday camp in the summer each year. There were lots of other children left behind, but most of them could not talk, so it was very lonely. I especially missed Vova.

I tried not to think about it and to just be happy talking to the carers, but I kept wondering what Vova and the other children were doing, and wishing I could be there too.

When Vova came back from the camp he talked to me a lot about all the things he had been doing and how much he liked the volunteers who played with the children."

A HOLIDAY FROM CONTAMINATION

The holidays began in 1998 and have continued every summer. About 70 children from Zhuravichi travel right across Belarus from the eastern edge of the country to a beautiful area near the Polish border. Neman Sanatorium, or holiday camp, is situated in a part of Belarus untouched by the radiation from Chernobyl. CCP (UK) raises money to pay for extra food for the children and outings, and they arrange the transport. About 20 volunteers fly out from the UK to Belarus to work at the camp alongside the carers from Zhuravichi.

THREE WEEKS OF FUN

At the holiday camp the children have three weeks of painting, making masks, models and puppets, performing puppet shows, face painting, and participating in storytelling and musical sessions. Some of the children play basketball or football, and they take part in races and play catching games. Every evening there is either a disco or a film. Discos are a favourite activity, and the children who cannot walk love to be twirled around in their wheelchairs!

A variety of activities are organised so that every child can take part.

IRA SAYS ...

"One day Linda came to visit. Vova and I were taken in a minibus to Gomel, with one of my carers. We went to a nice house where Liena, Sasha and Greesha were living. They all used to live at Zhuravichi and they have disabilities, too. They were very nice to us. They gave us lots of good things to eat and we watched television with them. We stayed there for a night and then a doctor came to see us the next day. The doctor was very nice and friendly and asked me lots of questions which Vova helped me answer because I felt quite shy. Then we went back to Zhuravichi. I thought about the visit for days.

Linda came to see me again soon afterwards. I recited a poem for the visitors which I had learned with Vova. Then Linda said something to Raisa Ivanovna, our Director. The interpreter told me that in the summer (2002) I would be going to the holiday camp. I could not believe it, and I almost cried.

I was so excited the first time I went to the camp, I could not sleep the night before. We all got into the bus very early in the morning and set off with everyone very noisy and happy. It was a long journey and so much to see! I looked out of the window most of the time at the forests and fields, houses and farms, cows and horses.

2004: Ira at the summer camp with her friends and some of the volunteers.

We went through Minsk, our capital city. It was huge and very beautiful, and full of cars. I got tired from sitting up for so long, so I was able to lie down across the seats and sleep. Ludmilla Markovna looked after me on the journey and at the camp. She is very nice and kind.

It was nearly the end of the day when we got to the holiday camp. It was beautiful, lots of grass and trees. The British people were there to meet us and we all went inside for something to eat and drink. Then we went to bed early because we were all so tired."

RESPITE HOLIDAYS ABROAD

In 1991, doctors in Belarus appealed to the world for help in providing clean air holidays for their children.

Since then charities have arranged for many thousands of children to travel from Belarus to enjoy a few weeks of uncontaminated food, fresh air, relaxation and fun. The children go to stay with families in Italy, Spain, Germany, France, the Netherlands, the US and Canada, as well as to Britain and Ireland. Some young children are accompanied by their mothers.

Many adults and children in the contaminated areas suffer from a variety of infections due to weakened immune systems. Doctors say that just four weeks in a clean environment can help the children to stay healthy or complete their recovery from illness. The holidays make a great difference to the children's immune systems and remove the build-up of radioactive substances in their bodies.

Max from England (in the centre) with his friends from Belarus, Maxim, Andrei and Vadim, who are all in remission from cancer.

Interpreter Natalia (second from left) with Youlia, Natasha and Inna on a respite holiday in Wales in 2000.

A PSYCHOLOGICAL BOOST

Many of the children are in remission after treatment for cancer. Others may have had operations or chronic illnesses, or simply live in some of the more contaminated villages in the south and east of Belarus. Respite holidays provide a physical boost to the health of these children and teenagers, and are also of great importance psychologically. The children return to Belarus feeling stronger and happier, with photographs and memories of new experiences and new friends.

IRA SAYS ...

"The food at the camp was nice and we were often given fruit and sweets. The weather was lovely, the sun was shining nearly every day and we were outside most of the time. It was good just to sit outside under the trees.

I liked all the English volunteers, especially Laura and Glenda. They took me for walks through the forest and down by the river. I watched the other children play and I really enjoyed watching concerts and going to the disco. I went for treatment, and massage too, and that made me feel better.

What I liked best of all was playing Boogie-Woogie OK (the Belarussian version of the Hokey-Cokey). It was so good to be part of a big group, with everyone singing and laughing and Vova pushing me backwards and forwards in my wheelchair."

GLENDA TRACEY SAYS ...

"When I worked as a volunteer at the holiday camp, my first impression of Ira was one of sadness, but by the end of the holiday all I had for her was love. She gains so much happiness by watching the other children enjoying themselves – it shows in her smile and eyes.

I remember taking her for a walk in her wheelchair for the first time over rough ground. She was not too sure, so we took a strap from a suitcase and made a safety belt across the chair – then she was up for exploring the grounds of the sanatorium and many other new experiences. The first time that Ira spoke to me she just came out with the words 'cheeky monkey' an expression that I had been saying to her. After this she would say it often, and start to laugh!"

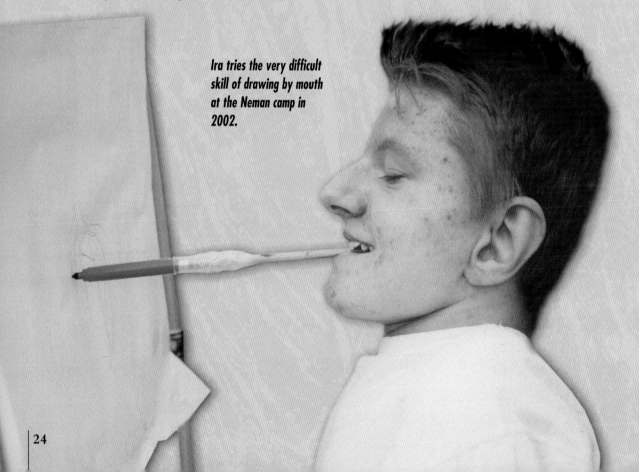

Ira tries the very difficult skill of drawing by mouth at the Neman camp in 2002.

At camp, the children are taken for walks in the woods, rides down the river on a boat, and on outings to the zoo or the park.

HELEN WALKER SAYS ...

"I was 16 the first time I volunteered at the holiday camp. The kids were amazing and I loved every minute of it. But when we had to say goodbye it was awful because we didn't know what life we were sending them back to. Was it cruel to give them all that love and then say, 'Goodbye, see you in a year'? I wasn't sure, until I visited them in their orphanage a few months later. All any of the children could say to me was, 'When are we going to the holiday camp again? Am I going? Are you going? Is she going?' It made me realise just how much of a difference the holidays make to the children's lives. I've now volunteered every summer for the past six years."

HELPING CHERNOBYL'S CHILDREN

People who volunteer at the holiday camp play a vital role in giving the children a wonderful three weeks.

• Most volunteers are young people and include many medical and physiotherapy students. Some volunteers have worked with children or with people with special needs before, as teachers, play workers or physiotherapists.

• Other volunteers are just enthusiastic, caring people keen to make a difference to the lives of so many children.

• The holidays are sometimes life changing for the volunteers. Many have been inspired to change their college course or their job, so that they can work with children with special needs in the future.

• Having so many volunteers and carers at the camp means that the children with severe physical needs, like Ira, or with profound learning difficulties can enjoy one-to-one support in a way that would never be possible at a home like Zhuravichi.

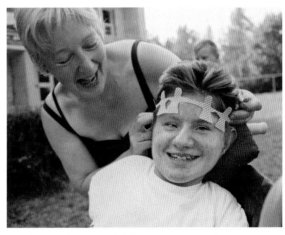

Holidays at the Neman holiday camp gave Ira the opportunity to meet lots of new people.

LINDA WALKER SAYS ...

"Ira's first holiday away from Zhuravichi opened her eyes to what she might be capable of if she was given the opportunity. When she returned to Zhuravichi she was desperate to be able to read and to have a chance to know more about the world outside the orphanage. In 2003, we arranged with Raisa, the Director of Zhuravichi, for some of the most disabled children to be taught by one of the Zhuravichi teachers, Ludmilla Markovna. That spring, Ira found herself in a classroom for the first time in her life and, later that year, we were able to arrange for her to go to live at the Rechitsa Boarding School, near to the city of Gomel."

IRA SAYS ...

"After I came back from my first holiday it seemed very quiet in my room at Zhuravichi.

My head was so full of stories about my new friends and the things I had done – I was bursting to talk about the holiday.

Ira loved to be read fairytales, but she wanted to be able to read them on her own.

I liked to sit in the corridor so I could sometimes chat to children from other parts of the building, because the children in my group could not really talk. Sometimes Natalia Nicolaevna came to talk to me. Natalia was my favourite carer, but then she became Deputy Director.

I was very happy when I started to have lessons with Ludmilla Markovna. She read me stories, and taught me to count, and I learned to read new words every day.

One day Natalia came to tell me I was going to leave Zhuravichi and go to live at Rechitsa Boarding School. I was upset to think of leaving Natalia and Ludmilla, but Vova was going too, and Peter, and Ghenya and Alina. And I would meet some of my friends from the holiday again.

Ludmilla Markovna with some of her pupils at Zhuravichi.

It was exciting and frightening at the same time.

I would miss everyone at Zhuravichi, but I wanted to go to study."

LUDMILLA MARKOVNA SAYS ...

"I soon found that it was a pleasure to teach Ira. She had a hunger for information and loved to listen to stories about people and relationships. When we looked at pictures she wanted to know everything about them. Ira liked to play with words and syllables. Lots of children find it hard to learn all the different endings on Russian words, and foreigners hate it! But Ira just loves the sound of words.

It was rewarding to teach Ira. It was not like taking water in a sieve, the work brought good fruit, and her face would shine with happiness when she thanked me for teaching her."

EDUCATION IN BELARUS

In Belarus, most children start school at six years old. In many schools, especially in country villages, the building is not big enough to accommodate all the pupils at once. Half the children start school early, at 8:00am, and finish in the early afternoon. Then a second shift starts and goes on into the evening. Children in Belarus are expected to take school very seriously. They study hard, rarely misbehave in school and have lots of homework. Many schools in contaminated areas stayed open after the Chernobyl accident, but the pupils were not allowed to play outside if the playground was radioactive.

This school in a contaminated part of Belarus was abandoned after the local population was evacuated.

SPECIAL NEEDS EDUCATION

In the past, education for children with special needs was not of a very high standard in Belarus. Children were assessed at five years old and could be judged as having 'oligophrenia' – few brains. This meant that they could never go to an ordinary school and as adults, employers would be reluctant to offer them jobs because of their 'problem'. Sometimes the children did not have learning difficulties at all, but had just had a bad start in life because of parents who were alcoholic or uncaring. It would be very unlikely that these children would be re-assessed and moved to a mainstream school. Children with more severe disabilities were often pronounced unteachable. There is now a law in Belarus that says that all children must be taught.

Living with Chernobyl – *Ira's Story*

IRA SAYS ...

"When I went to camp for the second time (in the summer of 2003), I knew I would soon be moving to Rechitsa School. I spent as much time as I could with girls from the school and made some friends. (Children from the Rechitsa Boarding School also go to the Neman holiday camp.) Just a week after we got back to Zhuravichi, we left for Rechitsa. The five of us (Ira, Vova, Peter, Ghenya and Alina) were dressed in our best clothes, we said goodbye to our friends and then we were put into the minibus for the journey to the school. I cried when I said goodbye to Natalia Nicolaevna, and she cried, too. The journey to Rechitsa took two hours and I felt sad all the way.

When we arrived we were quickly put into the isolation room. A doctor told us it was in case we had any illnesses which we might give to the other children. I wanted to see the girls I knew from the holiday and to have my first lesson, but we had to stay in this room for a week. I wondered if it would have been better to stay at Zhuravichi.

One morning we were all taken from the isolation room to the school hall. This is a very big room and all the children in the school were there. The carers gave me a wheelchair and I watched some of the children singing. Then I was taken to a classroom where I met my teacher. There were about eight other children in the class, but none of them could speak. I felt very shy, and when the teacher asked me questions, I just said, 'yes' or 'no' or 'OK.'"

ELENA VALERIEVNA SAYS ...

"I was Ira's first teacher when she came to Rechitsa. It took two or three weeks before Ira would really talk to us. Eventually she relaxed and started to answer

Ira and Vova with their new classmates at Rechitsa in November, 2004. There are 21 teachers at the school and 30 carers who help the children with their homework as well as their personal care.

our questions about how she felt, and what she wanted. It seemed she spent most of the time in bed at Zhuravichi. She told me she was worried that she was going to stay in the quarantine bed at Rechitsa! Now Ira has a nice bed, with a special, thick mattress, in a room she shares with five other girls. We gave her a bedside table and put a framed picture

of her on the wall. She was so pleased. Then she started to 'defrost'.

Recently, Ira was moved to a new class where all the children can speak. At the moment she is below the level of the other children in her new class, so she is like a sponge, absorbing everything!"

THE RECHITSA BOARDING SCHOOL

The pupils at the Rechitsa Boarding School are taught on a national mainstream programme. The children with learning difficulties follow an adapted special needs programme – all the children are encouraged to work as hard as they can. Sports, gymnastics, drama, art and music are also important at Rechitsa, and the children's talents in all these areas are recognised and developed.

Ira sits in on a sewing class at the Rechitsa school.

The children at Rechitsa range in age from 5 to 18 years old.

SOCIAL ORPHANS

There is a total of 106 children in the school at Rechitsa. Half of them never see their parents – they are what are know as 'social orphans'. This can mean that the parents have abandoned the children because of their disabilities (as in the case of Ira) or that the children have been taken away from parents who have severe alcohol problems. Living with poverty and anxiety about health problems, disabilities and what the future will hold has led to alcoholism becoming a widespread problem in the regions affected by the Chernobyl disaster. Vodka is a very cheap drink in this part of the world and the situation was initially made worse by official advice that, 'Vodka helps to protect you from radiation'.

CHAPTER FOUR: Ira's Life Today

Millions of people from Belarus, the Ukraine and parts of Russia, live with the consequences of the Chernobyl disaster every day of their lives. At places such as Zhuravichi and Rechitsa however, the accident and its effects are very rarely discussed. The staff feel the children have enough to worry about coping with their disabilities and coming to terms with what a difficult future is ahead of them.

IRA SAYS ...

"I still can't believe there is really going to be a book about me. My friends are all quite excited, and I hope they will all be in the book, too. I like looking at books about other children and hearing their stories. And now children will be able to read about me. I never imagined such a thing could be possible!

Ira in November, 2004. Some of the children's clothes are bought by the school. Overseas charities also send aid to schools and orphanages in Belarus, including lots of bright, colourful clothes!

Ira with her friends Luba (on the left) and Tanya. Unlike many wheelchair users Ira cannot use her arms to move her chair around. She relies on her friends and carers to push her everywhere.

I like to see myself in photographs. When we chose a picture for the wall in my room, my friends said they liked the ones with me smiling best. They were right, so now I always try to smile when someone takes my picture.

I always like to dress up in pretty clothes – have a bow put in my hair, wear something fluffy. I like skirts, and my favourite colour is red. I wore my red skirt for a lot of the photos for this book. I like to wear perfume and sometimes at the holiday camp the volunteers put make-up on me and colours on my nails. It made me feel very grown-up.

At Rechitsa, my friends Luba and Tanya help me to look pretty. It is exciting when visitors come. We all get dressed up and look as smart as we can."

BELARUS TODAY – HEALTH

Government resources in Belarus are still overstretched when it comes to coping with orphans and disabled children.

• Belarussian hospitals lack resources – from sterile needles and nappies, to expensive medicines and incubators for maternity wards.

• There has been an 80 per cent increase in disabled births in the Gomel region, even though women are encouraged to terminate pregnancies if any damage to the foetus is suspected.

• The World Health Organisation (WHO) predicts that one third of all Gomel region inhabitants aged 0 to 4 years at the time of the Chernobyl accident, will develop thyroid cancer in their lifetime. This will mean 50,000 cases in this one area of Belarus alone. Some radiation experts put the figure even higher at a predicted 100,000 cases.

• A UNICEF analysis of Belarussian health statistics showed that between 1990 and 1994, disorders of the nervous system in children increased by 43 per cent, cardiovascular diseases by 43 per cent, gastrointestinal diseases by 28 per cent, disorders of bone, muscle and connective tissue by 62 per cent and diabetes by 28 per cent.

• It has been internationally recognised that cases of breast cancer in the Gomel region have doubled.

Living with Chernobyl – *Ira's Story*

"I enjoy summertime best, when it is warm and we can spend lots of time outside. My friends push me around, or we sit under a tree and talk. You don't have to wear lots of clothes in the summer and I am much more comfortable. It is too cold to be outside in the winter and my wheelchair is too hard to push in the snow. I like animals. We have a cat called Malysh and a dog, Sharik, in our school yard, and I like to feed them with pieces of my bread. We also have fish in the aquarium, which I enjoy watching, and a hamster.

There are lots of activities at Rechitsa. I like pop music, especially fast music, and I love to go to the disco. We have lots of discos at the holiday camp and also here in school. Last Sunday, I was reading a book with Galina, my carer. I was enjoying the book, but when they put the music on in the hall and Galina asked if I wanted to keep reading or go to the disco, it wasn't hard to decide. I went straight to the disco! I try to move to the music, but I can't move much on my own, so I like it when someone swings my wheelchair in time to the music. It is fun when the grown-ups dance.

I like watching TV. We get to watch television every afternoon or evening and I love to see concerts and musical films. My favourite film is called Clone – it is about friends. I like to listen to people reading fairytales, too.

I like any food, but my favourites are fried meat and sausage, and bread and butter. My favourite lunch is 'draniki'. It is made from grated potatoes and meat. I also like fruit and chocolates and sweets. We usually get some sweets at the weekend. The food is nice here – tastier than it was at Zhuravichi.

One of the carers at Rechitsa feeds Ira as she cannot use her hands at all.

My favourite subjects in school are reading and reciting poems. I like to learn poems by heart, and I also enjoy studying Russian, but I find Belarussian really hard. Music lessons are fun and I quite like maths, but reading is definitely my favourite subject.

I am learning about religion. We have a priest who comes into school and I like to listen to him. Some of the children talk about God a lot. But I just listen. I don't think God can change my life.

I like it here. I am happy. But I still miss Natalia Nicolaevna and Ludmilla Markovna."

A TYPICAL DAY AT RECHITSA

The children wake up at 7:30am, get washed and dressed and have breakfast in the canteen at about 8:30am. Lessons take place between 9:00am and 1:30pm. At the end of the morning the children go for lunch in the canteen. In the afternoon it is homework time. Ira's friend, Luba, has three or four hours of homework to do every day. Ira does not have so much work to do, but she practises reciting poems and a carer helps her with her reading. In the evening, after a meal at 7:00pm the children sit with friends and chat, listen to music or watch films on TV until they are ready for bed.

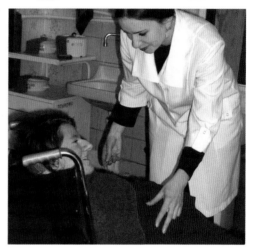

Doctors are a permanent part of the staff at Rechitsa. Ira has regular massage and heat therapy to ease her back pains.

Lunchtime in the canteen.

MEALTIMES AT RECHITSA

At Rechitsa the children eat their meals in the canteen. A typical breakfast is baked cottage cheese with potatoes and some salad. The children usually have soup at lunchtime, followed by pasta or potatoes with pork or chicken, and locally grown vegetables. Sometimes in the summer there is fruit to eat, but in winter this is a very rare treat.

IRA SAYS ...

"The children here at Rechitsa are very nice and kind. They treat me well. They take me where I ask them to, they put the television on for me and they get the carer to come if I need her.

I have lots of friends. When I was younger I liked to play school with my special friend, Vova. I was always the teacher. Sometimes we learned poems together. I would say one line, then Vova would say the next. We still spend a lot of time together as Vova is at the same school as me.

Here at Rechitsa, my best friends are the girls I share my room with, Luba and Tanya. I like to sit in the bedroom with Luba and Tanya and just chat. We talk about other friends, about what we have done in class and about the teachers."

VOVA SAYS ...

"When we were little I used to push Ira about. I also helped to feed her sometimes. If I did anything wrong, like feeding her too fast, she used to shout at me. It upset me because I was only trying to be helpful. I think Ludmilla Markovna talked to Ira about it, and then she became more patient. After that we used to play games where Ira was the carer or teacher and she used to order me about then too, but that was just for fun!"

Ira with her friends Luba and Tanya in their bedroom at Rechitsa, November 2004.

Luba, Tanya and Ira with some of the younger children in the Rechitsa playroom.

ABOUT IRA

During the preparation for this book Liena Fedarchuk (who works with CCP (UK) in Gomel) spoke to many people who have known Ira over the years. Everyone had something to say about Ira that they wanted included in the book!

"Ira is very talkative, but she never says anything bad about people. She never interrupts and would not shout. She is tactful, to put it in one word." (Ludmilla Markovna)

"In general, if Ira does not like something, she would rather keep silent about it, than say anything negative. Though Ira has a disability, she is kind towards other people and always smiles. I think she takes the world around her very positively and is always very appreciative. We went for a walk outdoors recently and I treated her to an apple – it was enough to make her happy." (Elena Valerievna, Ira's teacher at Rechitsa Boarding School)

"Ira has a very strong character, and is a very purposeful person. She wants to live and she lives in the present." (Deputy Head, Rechitsa Boarding School)

"Ira can be happy about a single day. If there is something good – then she is happy. If not, she might not even think about it tomorrow. Ira has a thirst for life and takes the life as it is today." (Galina, Ira's carer at Rechitsa Boarding School)

Liena Fedarchuk reads Ira the first draft of the book, translating the English text into Russian.

IRA SAYS ...

"Some days I think about my mother. I understand why she could not look after me, but I wish I could see her. I sometimes see a TV programme called Where are they now? *It helps people to find each other. I was hoping that my mother could be found through the programme, but my teacher said no-one knows an address for her, so it is too difficult.*

Some of the children here (at Rechitsa) have mothers who come to visit them and some have fathers, too. I am happy for them when their mums come to visit and I like to talk to the parents, but it makes me feel empty.

I hope my mother is still alive. Maybe one day I will meet her."

LUDMILLA MARKOVNA SAYS ...

"All our children (at Zhuravichi) who are able to speak, and understand what is happening around them, are desperate to talk about their family. Often they ask, 'Why is my mum not coming back for me? What does she do? What is her job?' So we use imagination to talk

Ira at the Rechitsa Boarding School, November 2004.

Ira in 1999, dressed up for visitors. The staff at Zhuravichi became Ira's family, and she liked to talk with them about their husbands and children.

to the children about their families.

Ira has never had any fantasies about her mother. She is a more rational girl.

A few years ago, I was in the eye hospital and met a blind woman from the next ward who was originally from Tihinichi village, near Rogachev. Ira's mum was supposed to have come from that village.

The woman told me about her severely disabled daughter who died. So, being a Sherlock Holmes in my heart, I thought for a while that she could have been Ira's mother. But then it appeared that the lady's name was Pirozhkova, while Ira's was Rozhkova."

BELARUS TODAY – THE SOCIAL AND ECONOMIC COST

The projected total cost to the economy of Belarus for the first 30 years after the accident (1986–2015) in lost production and the cost of dealing with the aftermath of the disaster, will be US$235 billion. This is the equivalent of 32 annual budgets.

• In the contaminated areas of Belarus, 54 large agricultural and forestry enterprises have had to close, together with nine industrial enterprises and 22 raw material deposits.

• Most of the people who have left the affected areas (and are still leaving) are young families. There is now a shortage of teachers and doctors, and companie and farms are closing due to a lack of skilled workers.

• Farming is no longer profitable for many in contaminated regions, despite financial help from the government. Even if produce has been strictly monitored and is deemed safe, it is difficult to sell.

• In 1986, the population of Gomel was increasing by 8 per cent per year. Now the birth rate is dropping and mortality has increased. In 2000, the population in the region shrank by 5.1 per cent.

CHAPTER FIVE: The Chernobyl Children

No-one knows how many children have been born severely disabled as a result of the Chernobyl accident. All we can say for sure is that, even though fewer children are being born in regions such as Gomel, the number of children born with disabilities has significantly increased. Ira is now 16 years old. She knows that her life will never be easy and that she will always need people to look after her.

LINDA WALKER SAYS ...

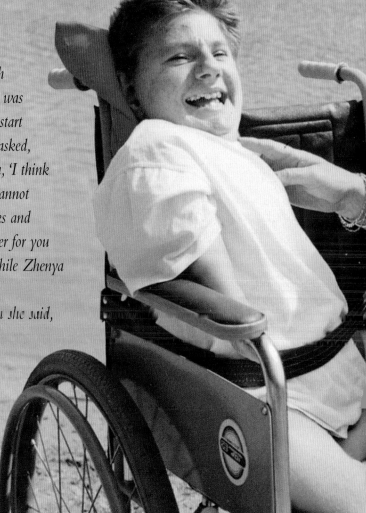

"One of Ira's carers at Rechitsa told us this story about a discussion that was had one day in class... Zhenya, one of the boys at Rechitsa, was about to have a throat operation, so we talked with the children about it. Ira asked what the operation was for. So I told her there is a hope that Zhenya can start talking, he might be better after the operation. Ira asked, 'Is there no operation that can help me?' I told Ira, 'I think not, but you can be happy that even though you cannot walk and write, you are able to talk. Zhenya walks and writes, but is not able to talk. In a way, it is simpler for you as you can say what you would like to happen, while Zhenya has to use gestures.'

Ira was very quiet for about 15 minutes. Then she said, 'You know, you're right.' I could not understand what she was talking about so I went and sat near her. Ira said, 'Nothing, no operation can help me, but I feel good. I am happy that I can speak.'

FAMILY HOME 2000

When young, disabled people leave orphanages they usually move on to adult boarding institutions where there is often very little for the residents to do. In the year 2000, CCP (UK) set up a small home where four young adults with physical disabilities (Liena, Greesha, Sasha and Sveta) could live in a family environment. They have learned to cook and look after themselves, and they are all learning trades which will help them to become more independent in the future.

Ira assessed her real abilities. She understands that nothing can help her, so she does not upset herself about it. She does not feel that God took any abilities off her. I think Ira believes that we are all different. She is not disabled, not defective, but individual. She is like she is."

IRA SAYS ...

"I don't really think about what will happen in the future. I know I will leave Rechitsa and go to another home, but I don't know where. Sometimes I think about being at Zhuravichi and being in a cot where none of the children around me could speak. I feel very lucky to be here at Rechitsa.

I am happiest when I do something and it is successful. But if I fail in something, I do not panic or get upset. I try to believe tomorrow will be a better day. For a while I would say, 'I cannot do that today.' So, my teacher at Rechitsa said to me, 'We need to conquer the cannot'. Now when there is a difficulty, I say, 'Let's conquer the cannot!'"

Because Ira made such a late start to her studies, Rechitsa Boarding School is happy to let her stay with them until she is 20. After that, CCP (UK) is hoping that it will be possible for Ira to move into their 'Family Home 2000', in Klimovka, just outside Gomel.

Ira enjoying her first holiday in 2002 at the Neman holiday camp. She is with volunteer, Glenda Tracey.

LIVING WITH THE RADIATION MONSTER

In 2006, it will be 20 years since the Chernobyl accident, but time has not been a healer for the people of the Chernobyl region. Many children living in the affected areas in Belarus, the Ukraine and Russia think a great deal about Chernobyl and worry about the effect it will have on their future lives. Tamara was 12 years old and lived in a village called Uvaravichi, near to the city of Gomel, when she travelled to the north of England for a holiday. She wrote a card to thank her host family for the visit saying, 'It seems to me that Chernobyl is like a great big monster trying to destroy us and the English families are our fairy godmothers helping to protect us from the radiation monster.'

A painting by teenagers in Belarus. The monster represents Chernobyl eating up the beautiful world.

TOMORROW'S CHERNOBYL CHILDREN

Today, doctors in the most contaminated parts of Belarus report that only 10 per cent of children are born completely healthy. Teenagers living in these areas are very frightened about what will happen when they get married and have children of their own. Many young people seek the opportunity to go and live abroad, where they hope they can improve their health and where their children will have a better chance of being born healthy in the future. Young men and women who were little children at the time of the accident are now becoming parents. Many young women are experiencing problems during pregnancy or labour, and there has been a rise in the number of children born with genetic defects.

NO END IN SIGHT

Many children still live in tiny rural villages, sometimes just a few kilometres from the Chernobyl plant. In the early years after the accident, people were very anxious about the effects of radiation, especially on their children, and they tried hard to find non-contaminated food to eat. However, it is hard for parents and carers to be vigilant for many years about a hazard that they cannot see, taste or smell. Many poor families have started to collect mushrooms in the forests again and shoot wild animals to supplement their diet. These foods are very high in caesium-137 and this is absorbed into the children's bodies. Eating contaminated food day after day causes the cumulative dose of radiation inside the body to grow. Children living in these conditions may not be ill yet, but their future is bleak if they continue to live in such a dangerous environment.

HELPING THE CHERNOBYL CHILDREN

Charities from all over the world continue to help children in the affected regions. They deliver humanitarian aid, bring children out of Belarus, the Ukraine and Russia for recuperative holidays, and help to support orphanages or hospitals;

Mothers and children at a hostel run by the Minsk cancer charity 'Children in Trouble'. Families stay at the hostel while children are undergoing cancer treatment in Minsk.

often sending out teams of volunteers to work on building projects. Many of the children who enjoy respite holidays are in remission from leukaemia or cancer. Holidays abroad are specially important for these children, particularly in their teens, when many fall ill for a second or third time, and the death rate is very high. A happy, healthy summer holiday may give them a better chance of survival.

The small 'family' home for young disabled children set up by CCP (UK) in Rogachev, Belarus. Papa Sergei on the right of the photograph has become the children's legal guardian. The children are cared for by 'aunties'.

CHERNOBYL CHILDREN'S PROJECT (UK)

The charity CCP (UK) helps children in Belarus and is one of the many organisations dedicated to improving the lives of children affected by the Chernobyl disaster. They work closely with homes for children with disabilities (such as the Abandoned Babies' Home, Zhuravichi orphanage and Rechitsa Boarding School).

CCP (UK) aid convoys deliver medical aid, school equipment, disability aids, toys, toiletries, nappies and bedding.

CCP (UK) have established a small 'family' home where young disabled adults can gain some independence, and they have set up a home for disabled children, where a small number of children live with 'aunties' (carers) as a proper 'family'.

CCP (UK) fund children's hospice care and organise training for hospice nurses. They have also run a training programme to help orphanage staff foster children into local families.

In 2004, CCP (UK) opened a centre in Gomel where severely disabled children who are cared for by their families can stay, while their families have a break.

Many of these projects have been established in close co-operation with the local authorities in the Gomel region who are enthusiastic about creating a better future for children with special needs.

CHAPTER SIX: The Future

The Chernobyl disaster has directly or indirectly affected the lives of nine million people in Belarus, the Ukraine and Russia – at least three million of those are children. Following the Chernobyl accident, fears that there could be another disaster of this magnitude, led to many countries around the world phasing out their nuclear power programmes during the late 1980s and 1990s.

French soldiers dressed in decontamination suits measure radioactivity levels during a drill that simulated a nuclear accident.

THE ULTIMATE ENERGY SOURCE

In the 1950s and 1960s, the world looked to nuclear power as a cheap, renewable source of energy. Just a kilogram of uranium could power a whole city, without producing any of the pollution effects associated with burning fossil fuels. However, as the nuclear industry grew, so did concerns about safety. Scientists learned that, even in small doses, radiation can cause cancer and the disposal of fuel rods, which stay radioactive for thousands of years, became an evermore worrying problem. In the aftermath of the Chernobyl disaster, huge public and political pressure, and the costs of new design and safety rules, curtailed the expansion of the nuclear power industry worldwide.

THE FUTURE FOR NUCLEAR POWER

Today, many in large, industrialised countries, such as the USA, see renewed investment in nuclear power as the only way forward in a world where energy sources are needed that will not produce greenhouse gases. However, many scientists point out that the nuclear fuel cycle does in fact produce carbon dioxide.

In Belarus, a desperately poor country that has to import nearly all of its energy, there are calls for the country to build its own new, modern nuclear power stations. Russia currently has 30 nuclear reactors in operation and is planning

The 'Memory Room' at a children's hospice in Minsk, Belarus.

During that time, an even longer-lasting solution will have to be found.

THE HEALTH IMPACTS

The full impact of the Chernobyl accident on the health of the people living in the affected regions is impossible to quantify. Even though doctors know that exposure to radiation will cause cancer, genetic mutations and many other medical conditions, there is no definitive way to prove whether disabilities and illness are due to radiation or some other cause

eight new ones, and the Ukraine remains committed to nuclear power, relying on nuclear energy for 45 per cent of its electricity needs. In the Ukraine, there are currently 13 nuclear power stations in operation with two new plants soon to be completed – despite warnings from overseas nuclear experts that defects could affect the safety of the new plants.

THE SARCOPHAGUS

At the Chernobyl power station reactor No. 4 remains enclosed in its reinforced, concrete sarcophagus. Hastily built and potentially unstable, the sarcophagus was only ever designed to last 20 to 30 years. In 2003, the Russian Atomic Energy Minister, Alexander Rumyantsev, reported that the structure could collapse at any time. An internationally funded project to build a new 100-metre high, 20,000-tonne steel shelter is now underway. The new shelter should be completed by 2008 and will contain the No. 4 reactor for at least 100 years.

The concrete sarcophagus that was built to hold Chernobyl power station's No. 4 nuclear reactor in 1986.

A CCP (UK) aid convoy drives across Europe to deliver humanitarian aid to Belarus.

The number of casualties therefore remains controversial, but experts now agree that the Chernobyl disaster caused many cancers and, in particular, thyroid cancer. The full medical impact of Chernobyl will not be known until at least 2016.

INTERNATIONAL AID

Due to the initial secrecy surrounding the accident (when the Ukraine was still part of the Soviet Union), it was 1989 before the full magnitude of the disaster became clear to the international community. In 1990, an 'Inter-Agency Task Force on Chernobyl' was established by the United Nations (UN) to raise funds and manage projects to mitigate the consequences of the Chernobyl accident in the affected states. Since 2001, aid projects have focused on medical programmes for the people most affected (women, children and liquidators) and projects that 'help people to help themselves' through economic aid and practical assistance in dealing with radioactive contamination. Many healthcare projects are also currently in operation, with the emphasis on early diagnosis and treatment of thyroid cancer and other cancers in children (these are often jointly funded by governments and charities). The UN estimates that tens of billions of dollars are still needed to address the disaster's aftermath and to help the millions living in contaminated areas.

NON-GOVERNMENTAL HELP

Around the world, many charities and non-governmental groups are raising money and working directly with the people of Belarus, the Ukraine and Russia. To date, these charitable organisations have arranged for more than half a million children to travel abroad for respite holidays. Across Europe, 38 cities and communities are twinned with places in the Chernobyl region. These cities work with their Chernobyl twins to help improve the lives of people living with the ongoing after-effects of the disaster.

THE CHERNOBYL REGION

Today, almost 400,000 people (environmental refugees) have had to leave their homes as a result of the Chernobyl accident. Over 2,000 towns and villages have been abandoned, bulldozed or buried. Despite official prohibition, at least 800, mostly older, people have returned to live in villages inside the 30 km exclusion zone. They choose to live with the dangers of radiation, rather than live in unfamiliar cities. Scientists predict it will not be safe to live in the exclusion zone until the year 2300. Areas in the Chernobyl region contaminated with plutonium will be uninhabitable forever.

LIVING WITH CHERNOBYL

In the future, it is vital that governments around the world maintain a commitment to the residents of the towns and villages around Chernobyl. It is essential that greater research into the health effects of the accident take place and that every effort is made to ensure that the Chernobyl No. 4 reactor is made completely safe for the future.

Today, over 430 nuclear power stations are currently in operation worldwide, with more under construction. At the time of the Chernobyl accident, Soviet government officials said that the odds of a meltdown at the Chernobyl plant were one in 10,000 years.

The disaster is summed up in the following 2001 statement from five scientists at the Ukraine Ministry of Health – 'The Chernobyl radiation accident is undoubtedly the greatest environmental catastrophe in the history of mankind.' The world must never forget the children of Chernobyl, the generations yet to come and the terrible events of Saturday, 26 April, 1986.

Belarussian teenagers and volunteers at the Neman holiday camp in 2000.

HOW YOU CAN HELP

1. ORGANISE A FUNDRAISER

Funds are desperately needed to continue helping children like Ira:

£20 will transport 10 boxes of humanitarian aid to Belarus on one of CCP (UK)'s trucks.

£60 will pay the salary of one carer for one month at CCP (UK)'s new respite care home.

£200 will pay one child's airfare from Belarus to the UK for a holiday which will boost their immune system.

2. ORGANISE A COLLECTION OF TOYS

Lego and other educational toys are always desperately needed by orphanages and hospitals. See www.chernobyl-children.org.uk.

3. BECOME A HOST FAMILY

Perhaps your family would like to welcome a couple of children from Belarus into your home for two weeks next summer and give them a break from their radioactive environment.

4. BE INFORMED OF THE ISSUES AND RAISE AWARENESS

Sign up with one of the organisations on page 47 to receive regular newsletters, then pass on the information to as many people as possible.

5. SEND A PICTURE TO IRA

Send a picture of yourself, your family and friends to Ira. Then Ira and her friends will know that you have read her book and enjoyed it. Send these to CCP (UK) – see page 47 for address details.

GLOSSARY

CAESIUM-137 A radioactive isotope widely distributed following the Chernobyl accident. Caesium-137 has a 'half-life' of 30 years.

CORE A tough, steel container at the heart of a nuclear reactor. Nuclear fission takes place inside the core producing the heat which, when converted to steam, powers turbines that produce electricity. A core contains about 4,000 rods of uranium fuel.

FUEL RODS A rod containing uranium used as the fuel in a nuclear reactor. Used fuel rods remain dangerously radioactive.

HALF-LIFE The time taken for the radioactivity of an isotope to fall to half its value. For example, caesium-137 has a 'half-life' of 30 years. This means after 30 years, half of the original quantity of radioactive atoms in a quantity of caesium-137 will have decayed. After another 30 years, a quarter of the original amount will remain.

IODINE-131 A radioactive isotope widely distributed following the Chernobyl accident. Iodine-131 has a 'half-life' of 8 days, so was dangerous in the immediate aftermath of the accident, but no longer represents a problem. Iodine-131 is absorbed by the thyroid gland which cannot distinguish it from stable (non-radioactive), natural iodine which is needed by the body.

ISOTOPE An isotope is a form of an element that has most of the characteristics of the pure element, but differs in its properties and its radioactivity.

LEUKAEMIA A form of cancer affecting the blood producing cells in bone marrow. Radioactive strontium-90 is deposited in the bones and is thought to cause leukaemia.

MELTDOWN When the fuel rods in a nuclear reactor overheat and melt.

NUCLEAR FISSION The process by which atomic nuclei are split apart. In nuclear fission, radioactive atoms shoot out neutrons which split the nuclei of other atoms, releasing large amounts of energy which in turn release more neutrons to create a chain reaction.

PLUTONIUM One of the radionuclides distributed following the Chernobyl accident. Some plutonium isotopes have a 'half-life' of up to 24,000 years.

RADIOACTIVE Radionuclides are unstable and when they decay, they give off various forms of radiation. These unstable atoms are termed radioactive. Some radioactive substances such as uranium and radium are found in nature. Others, such as strontium and plutonium, are produced artificially in laboratories or nuclear reactors.

RADIOACTIVITY The emission of radiation caused by the disintegration of unstable atomic nuclei.

REACTOR An installation at a nuclear power plant where the nuclear fission reaction takes place.

SOVIET UNION The Union of Soviet Socialist Republics (USSR), a former federation of 15 communist republics occupying the northern half of Asia and part of Eastern Europe. The USSR was created from the former Russian Empire as a communist state in the aftermath of the Russian Revolution and the Russian Civil War. It was governed from its capital Moscow (now the capital of Russia). The USSR was the biggest country in the world and emerged as a superpower to rival the USA. Following many years of repression and economic failure, the USSR was formally dissolved in 1991, which led to a resurgence of nationalist feeling in the republics.

STRONTIUM-90 A radioactive isotope widely distributed following the Chernobyl accident. Strontium-90 has a 'half-life' of 30 years. Other strontium isotopes have 'half-lives' of up to 90 years.

TURBINE A device that spins and produces electricity.

UNICEF The United Nations Children's Fund, an agency of the UN established to help governments improve the health, lives and education of the world's children.

UNITED NATIONS (UN) An international organisation of countries set up in 1945 to promote international peace, security and co-operation. Some of its functions today include working on social, educational and health issues.

URANIUM A radioactive element whose isotopes are used as fuel in nuclear reactors. It is used to create plutonium which can be used in nuclear power and in atomic weapons.

FURTHER INFORMATION

CHERNOBYL CHILDREN'S PROJECT (UK)
Kinder House, Fitzalan Street, Glossop, Derbyshire, SK13 7DL, United Kingdom
www.chernobyl-children.org.uk

CHERNOBYL CHILDREN'S PROJECT INTERNATIONAL
217 East 86th Street, New York, NY 10028 United States of America www.ccp-intl.org

CHILDREN OF CHORNOBYL RELIEF FUND
A humanitarian organisation serving as a resource bridge between the Ukraine, the USA and the world community. www.childrenofchornobyl.org

INTERNATIONAL CHERNOBYL RESEARCH INFORMATION NETWORK (ICRIN)
An international communications platform on the long-term consequences of the Chernobyl disaster. www.chernobyl.info

UNICEF – To download the 2002 report, 'The Human Consequences of the Chernobyl Nuclear Accident' go to: www.undp.org/dpa/publications/chernobyl.pdf

WORLD INFORMATION SERVICE ON ENERGY (WISE)
This website contains lots of information on nuclear power and anti-nuclear struggles worldwide. www.antenna/nl/wise/

THE NUCLEAR ENERGY INSTITUTE (NEI)
The policy organisation of the nuclear energy and technologies industry. NEI participates in both the national (USA) and global policy-making process. www.nei.org